D0824133

Autograph manuscript of
String Quartet No. 15, Op.132:
Mvmt. V, mm. 158–163

Late String Quartets and the Grosse Fuge

Opp. 127, 130–133, 135

Ludwig van Beethoven

From the Breitkopf & Härtel Complete Works Edition

DOVER PUBLICATIONS, INC.
Mineola, New York

Copyright

Published in Canada by General Publishing Company, Ltd., 30 Lesmill Road, Don Mills, Toronto, Ontario.
Published in the United Kingdom by Constable and Company, Ltd., 3 The Lanchesters, 162–164 Fulham Palace Road, London W6 9ER.

Bibliographical Note

This Dover edition, first published in 1998, is an unabridged republication of six works from *Serie 6, Zweiter Band: Quartette für 2 Violinen, Bratsche und Violoncell* of *Ludwig van Beethoven's Werke. Vollständige kritisch durchgesehene überall berechtigte Ausgabe. Mit Genehmigung aller Originalverleger,* originally published by Breitkopf & Härtel, Leipzig, n.d. The Dover edition adds a frontispiece, an annotated list of contents with notes on the music, and new headings throughout.

International Standard Book Number: 0-486-40111-1

Manufactured in the United States of America
Dover Publications, Inc., 31 East 2nd Street, Mineola, N.Y. 11501

Contents

These six works were originally issued independently by three different firms, resulting in a mismatch between their dates of composition and the opus numbers assigned to the works by their publishers. Schott, Mainz, published Quartets Nos. 12 and 14; Arturia, Vienna, published No. 13 and the *Grosse Fuge;* Schlesinger, Berlin, published Nos. 15 and 16.

*See NOTES, p. viii

Late String Quartets and the Grosse Fuge

Opp. 127, 130–133, 135

Notes

STRING QUARTET No. 13, Op. 130
Movement VI: Finale / p. 59

Following the quartet's premiere in March 1826, the original finale—the *Grosse Fuge*—was criticized in print as being ". . . incomprehensible . . . a sort of Chinese puzzle . . ." In his biography, *Beethoven As I Knew Him,* Anton Schindler went on to report that ". . . Matthias Artaria . . . purchaser of the manuscript . . . offered to buy the fugue as a separate work if Beethoven would compose another finale in free style to put in its place. The master complied with this condition and wrote the movement that appeared in the published version of the work. This was his very last composition, and was written in November 1826." The *Grosse Fuge* was published separately, in 1827, as Op. 133 (*see below*).

STRING QUARTET No. 15, Op. 132
Movement III: "Heiliger Dankgesange" / p. 127

"The composition of Op. 132 was interrupted by a serious illness in April 1825, and an extraordinary 'Hymn of thanksgiving to the divinity, from a convalescent, in the Lydian mode' forms the central movement. Beethoven's intimations of mortality take the form of modal cantus firmus variations . . . alternat[ing] movingly with a purely tonal section entitled 'Feeling new strength' [m. 31]."

Grove, 1980: Vol. 2

STRING QUARTET No. 16, Op. 135
Movement IV / p. 155

"DER SCHWER GEFASSTE ENTSCHLUSS: Muss es sein? . . . Es muss sein!"

(*The Difficult Decision: Must it be? . . . It must be!*)

"We cannot know with certainty what prompted the master's serious joke, or joking seriousness. One explanation concerns Beethoven's housekeeper, who was given weekly expense money. It was often difficult for her to get it at the right time, for the master was not to be disturbed at his work. Old Frau Schnaps used to stand, waiting, at his desk, all dressed to go to market. Then would come Beethoven's question, sometimes even sung: 'Must it be?' to which the old woman would nod her head or stamp her foot and answer: 'It must be!' This joke was repeated almost every Saturday, amusing the master in a way that only the sly but faithful old servant could amuse him."

Adapted from Schindler, *Beethoven As I Knew Him* (Dover, 1996: 0-486-29232-0)

GROSSE FUGE [Great Fugue], Op. 133 / p. 161

The Breitkopf edition carried the following French inscription below the title:

"(Grande Fugue, tantôt libre, tantôt recherchée)"

[*Great Fugue, sometimes free, sometimes studied*]

To Prince Nikolai Golitsïn

String Quartet No. 12
in E-flat Major, Op. 127
(1823–4)

33
41
50
58
67
p
cresc.
dim.
f
pp
ten.
tr

Maestoso.
Allegro.
75
83
93
104
114
cresc.
dim.

124
132
Maestoso.
Allº
tr
ff
sf
f
p
142
151
161
cresc.

170
179
cresc.
cresc.
cresc.
cresc.
188
197
206
cresc.
cresc.
cresc.
cresc.
dim.
dim.
dim.
dim.
cresc.
cresc.
cresc.
cresc.

215
dim.
cresc.
f
223
p
cresc.
f
ten.
tr
233
1
245
255

264
p dolce
dim.
cresc.
273
dim.
p
pp
Adagio, ma non troppo e molto cantabile.
pp
cresc.
p
5
tr
10
pp

15
cresc.
p
dim.
cresc.
20
pp
24
dim.
tr
27
sf
31

34
sf
cresc.
37
p
dim.
Andante con moto.
pp
41
sempre stacc.
44
dim.
tr
46
cresc.

48
poco cresc.
poco cresc.
poco cresc.
poco cresc.
50
più cresc.
più cresc.
più cresc.
più cresc.
53
cresc.
cresc.
cresc.
cresc.
55
p dol.
p dol.
p dol.
p dol.
57
cresc.
cresc.
cresc.
cresc.
p
p
p
p

59
dim.
cresc.
61
Adagio molto espressivo.
68
cantabile
espressivo
75
Tempo I.
80

83
cantabile
cresc.
86
cresc.
rinf.
89
rinf.
cresc.
92
rf
cresc.
95
dim.
sotto voce
p
pp

99
pizz.
arco
cresc.
104
p
cresc.
109
p dolce
tr
cresc.
112
cresc.
p
115
cresc.
f
p

118
dim.
cresc.
121
pizz.
pp
cresc.
p
125
cresc.
ritard.
rit.
ten.
arco
Scherzando vivace.
pizz.
arco
pp
9
fp
f

19
26
35
40
47
tr
p
cresc.
f
1.
2.
pp
ff

54
cresc.
rf
ff
61
pp
f
67
Allegro.
75
Tempo I.
pp
Allegro.
Tempo I.
84
p
cresc.
sempre f

91
98
105
113
121
cresc.
1.
2.

126
tr
cresc.
dim.
132
tr
p
più piano
pp
138
Presto.
sempre pp
cresc.
148
f
pp
159
1.
2.
p cresc.
ff

169
181
192
cresc.
203
215

226
cresc.
ff
237
f
sf
249
261
dim.
p dim.
Tempo I.
pp
271
sempre pp
tr

279
pp
cresc.
f
fp
289
p
296
p cresc.
f
305
ff
311

317
cresc.
p
323
329
rinf.
ff
335
pp
f
341
Allegro.
Tempo I.
Allegro.

Tempo I.
352
pp
cresc.
sempre f
360
367
374
sf
p
tr
380
f

389
cresc.
395
401
dim.
più piano
407
Presto.
sempre pp
417

427
Tempo I.
pp
sempre pp
cresc.
ff
Finale.
sf
p
f
sul G
9
19
28

37
pp
sempre pp
45
sempre pp
cresc.
53
f
63
p
f
73
ff

81
90
99
110
119
f
p
pp
cresc.
sf
sempre p
ff

128
p
f
f
p
135
sempre p
cresc.
dim.
143
tr
pp
p
153
162
cresc.
p

171
f p cresc.
180
dim. pp
189
p dolce dolce
198
cresc. p f
206
p f

214
222
231
241
249
p
f
ff
dim.
ritar
pp
dan
do

Allegro con moto.
256
cresc.
pp
261
sempre pp
264
267
271

274
278
283
289
294
ff
sf
p
cresc.
f
ff non ligato
non ligato
pp
sempre pp

To Prince Nikolai Golitsïn

String Quartet No. 13
in B-flat Major, Op. 130
(1825–6)

Tempo I.
Allegro.
f non ligato
f non ligato
f non ligato
cresc.
cresc.

39
dim.
cresc.
dim.
cresc.
dim.
cresc.
dim.
cresc.
43
47
dim.
dim.
dim.
una corda
dim.
52
Corda C
sotto voce
59
pp ben marcato
ben marc.
pp
pp ben marcato
pp ben marcato

66
poco cresc.
poco cresc.
poco cresc.
poco cresc.
70
pp
pp
pp
pp
cresc.
cresc.
cresc.
cresc.
73
p
p
p
p
cresc.
cresc.
cresc.
cresc.
p
p
p
p
76
cresc.
cresc.
cresc.
p
p
p
80
cresc.
cresc.
cresc.
cresc.

83
86
89
92
97
1.
2.
Tempo I.
Allegro.
Adagio ma non troppo.
Allegro.
Adagio ma non troppo.
più p
pp
p cresc.
pp non ligato
cresc.
espressivo

104
Allegro.
sempre p
sempre p
non ligato
sempre p
sempre p
non ligato
110
116
122
128
dim.
pp
cresc.
f
dim.
pp
cresc.
non ligato
f
dim.
pp
cresc.
non ligato
f
dim.
pp
cresc.
non ligato
f

133
cresc.
136
ten.
ben marcato
140
non ligato
143
146
dim.

149
cresc.
cresc.
cresc.
cresc.
f
f
f
152
sf
sf
f
f
f
f
f
f
f
f
f
f
156
f
f
f
f
f
f
sf
sf
f
f
f
f
dim.
dim.
dim.
dim.
p
p
p
p
160
sotto voce
p
p
166
p
p
p
p

173
cresc.
p
179
pp ben marcato
186
poco cresc.
pp
190
non ligato
193

197
cresc.
cresc.
cresc.
cresc.
p
p
p
p
200
cresc.
cresc.
cresc.
cresc.
203
sf
206
ff
sf
209
p
dim.

Adagio ma non troppo.
214
cresc.
Allegro.
f non ligato
219
Adagio ma non troppo.
Allegro.
Adagio ma non troppo.
222
Allegro.
cresc.
227
231
sempre pp

Presto.
pp
8
cresc.
15
L'istesso tempo.
f
sf
21
1.
2.
p
27
pp

34
cresc.
41
1.
47
2.
dim.
L'istesso tempo.
ritar - dan - do
56
64

70
tr
pp sempre
pp sempre
pp sempre
pp sempre
77
84
p
91
cresc.
f
pp
pizz.
98
poco ritard.
arco
f in tempo

Andante con moto ma non troppo.
Poco scherzoso.
dolce
5
cresc.
8
cresc.
pizz.
11
arco
14

16
sempre pp
18
dim.
pp
cresc.
21
poco cresc.
dim.
p poco cresc.
23
cresc.
ten.
poco f
p cresc.
25
Cantabile.
p dolce

27
tr
poco f
mf
29
p
cresc.
31
pp
33
35
dim.

38
p dolce
p dolce
p dolce
p
sempre staccato
40
p
p
p
p
cresc.
cresc.
cresc.
stacc.
cresc.
43
cresc.
p
cresc.
stacc. p
pp
pizz.
arco
fp
46
49
pp

51
sempre pp
sempre pp
6
6
6
6
sempre pp
sempre pp
fp
fp
fp
fp
53
dim.
pp
cresc.
p
dim.
pp
cresc.
p
dim.
pp
cresc.
p
dim.
pp
cresc.
p
56
poco cresc.
dim.
p poco cresc.
dim.
58
pp
poco cresc.
dim.
p poco cresc.
dim.
pp
poco cresc.
dim.
p poco cresc.
dim.
pp
poc cresc.
dim.
p poco cresc.
dim.
cresc.
poco f
mf
ten.
p cresc.
mf
ten.
poco f
mf
sf
cresc.
poco f
mf
p cresc.
mf
poco f
mf
sf
cresc.
cresc.
poco f
mf
p cresc.
mf
poco f
mf
sf
pp
cresc.
poco f
mf
p cresc.
mf
poco f
mf
sf
61
p dolce
tr
p
p dolce
p dolce

63
cresc.
dolce
65
tr
non troppo presto
Tempo I.
67
p
pp
pizz.
sempre pp
arco
pizz
70
arco
73
più p

76
cresc.
mf
p
79
pp
sempre pp
82
dim.
85
p dolce
più p
87
f

Alla danza tedesca.
Allegro assai.
cresc.
dim.

44
p cresc.
f
dim.
p
cresc.
p cresc.
52
cress.
sempre p
dim.
60
69
78

86
p
p
p
p
cresc.
94
cresc.
cresc.
cresc.
102
110
118

126
136
144
cresc.
Cavatina.
Adagio molto espressivo.
sotto voce
8

16
cresc.
23
sotto voce
30
37
Beklemmt.
sempre pp
43

47
sotto voce
cresc.
p
sotto voce
54
cresc.
p
61
dim.
pp
Finale.
Allegro.
ten.
sempre stacc.
8

15
tr
pp
cresc.
24
1.
2.
35
sf
p
cresc.
38
dolce
46
f

53
dim.
60
cresc.
66
poco cresc.
dim.
74
ten.
cresc.
83

89
ff
dim.
1.
2.
97
p
pp
poco ritard.
in tempo
102
cresc.
112
121

130
cresc.
p
cresc.
dim.
cresc.
139
p
p cresc.
pp
cresc.
150
cresc.
p
p cresc.
159
p
pp
167
f
p
sempre p

173
sempre p
179
185
cresc.
cresc.
cresc.
cresc.
191
197
f
più f
f
più f
più f
f
più f

203
ff
ff
ff
ff
ff
ff
ff
ff
sempre staccato
sempre staccato
sempre staccato
sempre staccato
210
sf
sf
f
f
f
f
f
219
dim.
p
più
p
pp
pp
228
poco cresc.
poco cresc.
poco cresc.
poco cresc.
pp
pp
pp
237
tr

246
tr
cresc.
cresc.
cresc.
cresc.
253
sf
p
sf
p
sf
p
sf
p
tr
tr
261
pp
pp
pp
pp
cresc.
cresc.
cresc.
cresc.
268
sf
sf
sf
sf
p
cresc.
cresc.
cresc.
cresc.
sf
sf
sf
sf
sf
sf
cresc.
cresc.
sf
sf
276
sf
sf
sf
cresc.
dim.
dim.
dim.
dim.
dolce
dolce
dolce
dolce

283
cresc.
291
f
sf
297
dim.
p
304
311
poco cresc.
dim.
pp
ten.

320
cresc.
pp
cresc.
cresc.
cresc.
f
sf
326
sf
ff
332
dim.
p
338
poco ritard.
in tempo
poco ritard.
in tempo
poco ritard.
in tempo
347
cresc.
dim.
poco ritard.
in tempo
cresc.
poco ritard.
in tempo
cresc.
poco ritard.
in tempo
cresc.
cresc.
dim.
cresc.

355
364
373
382
392
cresc.
p
dim.
pp

401
p cresc.
p cresc.
p cresc.
p cresc.
p cresc.
p cresc.
410
dim.
dim.
dim.
dim.
pp
pp
pp
pp
418
cresc. poco a poco
cresc. poco a poco
cresc. poco a poco
cresc. poco a poco
424
al f
al f
al f
al f
più f
più f
più f
ff
ff
ff
ff
430

436
sf
dim.
pp
443
pp
sempre pp
449
pp
cresc.
455
sf
cresc.
460
cresc.
p
tr

465
cresc.
471
477
483
489
più p
pp
ff

To Baron Joseph von Stutterheim

String Quartet No. 14

in C-sharp Minor, Op. 131

(1826)

36
rfz
p
45
cresc.
p
54
f
p
più cresc.
60
rfz
dim.
p dolce
cresc.
p
67
dolce

77
86
94
101
107

113
cresc. dim. p più p pp
No.2. Allegro molto vivace.
125
in tempo
un poco ritard.
cresc.
130
138
p cresc.
146

155
dim.
cresc.
164
p
più p
pp
173
in tempo
poco rit.
cresc.
181
f
p
cresc.
sf
189
p

197
in tempo
cresc.
p espress.
poco rit.
p
206
cresc.
p
214
poco rit.
in tempo
cresc.
f
p
222
cresc.
230
f
p

243
dim.
p più p
pp
252
f
p
260
cresc.
sf
269
cresc.
p espress.
poco rit.
in tempo
278

286
cresc.
fp
f
p
294
cresc.
f
302
ff
p
310
mezza voce
pp
Nº 3. Allegro moderato.
322
f
p

324
Adagio.
più vivace
Adagio.
più vivace
328
cresc.
rinf.
cresc.
rf
cresc.
f
cresc.
rf
cresc.
f
cresc.
rf
cresc.
f
No. 4. Andante ma non troppo e molto cantabile.
337
p dolce
p dolce
pizz.
340
349
cresc.
cresc.
cresc.
cresc.
arco
pizz.

357
cresc.
cresc.
cresc.
cresc.
p
p
p
arco
366
cresc.
p
cresc.
cresc.
p
cresc.
p
cresc.
p
cresc.
cresc.
p
373
379
cresc.
cresc.
cresc.
cresc.
p
p
p
p
cresc.
cresc.
cresc.
cresc.
383
p cresc.
p cresc.
p cresc.
p cresc.
p dolce
p
p

387
cresc.
p
391
p cresc.
dim.
395
Più mosso.
pp
400
405

410
cresc.
415
420
p cresc.
425
Andante moderato e lusinghiero.
dolce
p dolce
430
cresc.
tr

436
dolce
dolce
cresc.
442
cresc.
448
454
459
Adagio.
pizz.
arco
pizz.

463
pizz.
arco
cresc.
pizz.arco
sf
468
pizz.
arco
dolce
473
477
481
cresc.
dim.

485
cresc.
dim.
489
Allegretto.
pizz.
492
p dol.
arco
501
510
1.
2.

517
Adagio ma non troppo e semplice.
sotto voce
sotto voce
sotto voce
sotto voce
521
cresc.
cresc.
cresc.
cresc.
p cantabile
p cantabile
p
p
525
non troppo marcato
529
cresc.
cresc.
cresc.
cresc.
p
p
p
p
poco cresc. p
poco cresc. p
poco cresc. p
poco cresc. p
533
pp
pp
pp
pp
f
pp
f
pp

537
cresc.
p
poco cresc.
541
f
pp
544
547
dim.
550
sotto voce

553
cresc.
dim.
556
cresc.
dim.
p
più p
morendo
560
ppp
Allegretto.
p dolce
p
sempre più allegro
cresc.
567
in tempo
dim. e ritard.
p più p
pp
cresc.
p
574
tr

577
580
Allegretto.
584
sempre più allegro
dolce
cresc.
dim. e rit.
in tempo
594
cantabile
599
semplice
pizz.

No. 5. Presto.
arco
cresc.
dim.
Molto poco adagio.
più p
un poco più adagio
pp
Tempo I.
ritard.
in tempo

656
p
cresc.
666
f
sf
1.
p
673
2.
piacevole
piacevole
683
pp
693
cresc.

703
cresc.
p
713
Ritmo di quattro battute.
724
Ritmo di quattro battute.
734
p cresc.
744
p cresc.

754
cresc.
cresc.
cresc.
cresc.
764
f
più f
ff
pizz.
pizz
pizz.
pizz.
arco
776
arco
p
f
786
cresc.
dim.
796

806
Molto poco adagio.
più p
Tempo I.
pp
un poco più adagio
815
in tempo
ritard.
f
824
p
cresc.
834
f
sf
piacevole
844

854
pp
864
cresc.
p
874
Ritmo di quattro battute.
884
895

904
p
cresc.
p cresc.
p
914
cresc.
924
f
più f
ff
pizz.
arco
sempre p
935
945

955
pp
sempre pp
965
Molto poco adagio.
un poco più adagio
976
Tempo I.
in tempo
ritard.
p
986
996

1006
cresc.
1016
dim.
Molto poco adagio.
più p
Tempo I.
pp
un poco più adagio
1026
in tempo
ritard.
f
1035
p
cresc.
1045
sf

1054
piacevole
piacevole
p cresc.
cresc.
cresc.
p cresc.
1064
cresc.
cresc.
cresc.
cresc.
pizz.
pizz.
pizz.
pizz.
1076
sul ponticello
arco
dim.
sul ponticello
sul ponticello
sul ponticello
arco
pp
dim.
1086
sempre pp
sempre pp
sempre pp
sempre pp
da capo per l'ordinario
da capo per l'ordinario
da capo per l'ordinario
da capo per l'ordinario
cresc.
1096
ff
ff
ff
ff
attacca

1106
Nº 6. Adagio quasi un poco andante.
cresc.
dim.
1117
1127
1134
Nº 7. Allegro.
1142

1149
p
p
p
p
p
p
p
1157
p
p
p
p
p
1165
p
cresc.
f
p
cresc.
f
p
cresc.
f
p
cresc.
f
1174
p
p
p
p
1181
p
cresc.
p
cresc.
ff
p
cresc.
ff
p
p
cresc.
ff

1188
poco riten.
in tempo
espress.
cresc.
1197
in tempo
espress.
poco riten.
ri - tar - dan - do
1207
cresc.
1216
1223
sempre f

1231
1238
1246
1253
1260
non ligato

1266
non ligato
cresc.
1272
non ligato
non ligato
1278
dim.
Ritmo di tre battute.
p
1284
p
pp
1290
cresc.
ff

1296
1302
1309
1316
1325
cresc.
cresc.
cresc.

1335
p
p
p
p
1341
cresc.
cresc.
cresc.
cresc.
1347
f
f
f
f
p
p
p
p
espress.
cresc.
poco riten.
in tempo
cresc.
cresc.
cresc.
p
p
p
1354
cresc.
cresc.
espress.
cresc.
poco riten.
cresc.
p
p
in tempo
p
p
cresc.
espress.
cresc.
poco riten.
cresc.
cresc.
in tempo
ri -
ri -
ri -
ri -
1362
tar - dan - do
tar - dan -
do
tar - dan -
do
tar - dan - do
p
in tempo
p
p
p
cresc.
cresc.
cresc.
cresc.
p
p
p
p

1373
cresc.
p
espress.
poco riten.
p in tempo
1380
in tempo
ri tar dan do
p in tempo
1390
pp
sempre pp
1399
cresc.
1405
f
p

1411
1421
1429
1436
1443
sempre f

1450
1458
non ligato
dim.
cresc.
1465
cresc.
1472
1478
Ritmo di due battute.

1485
1492
pp
1501
p
1508
Poco adagio.
semplice
espress.
espress.
semplice
espress.
1515
Tempo I.
cresc.
cresc.
cresc.
cresc.
ff

To Prince Nikolai Golitsïn

String Quartet No. 15
in A Minor, Op. 132
(1825)

30
37
42
48
54
cresc.
fp
non ligato
p dolce
più cresc.
dim.
teneramente
dolce

59
cresc.
non ligato
f
ff
63
p ligato
p lizato
cresc.
67
ff
sf
p
ri - tar - dan - do
cresc.
a tempo
f
75
pp
85
cresc.
f

92
99
109
118
124
cresc.
dim.
espressivo

30
Adagio.
Allegro.
38
45
cresc.
50
55
non ligato
non ligato
p dolce

60
p
più cresc.
più cresc.
più cresc.
più cresc.
65
dim.
p teneramente
dim.
p
dim.
dim.
p
p
70
cresc.
teneramente
p dolce
cresc.
p dolce
cresc.
p dolce
cresc.
p dolce
74
cresc.
non ligato
f
ff
cresc.
non ligato
f
ff
cresc.
f non ligato
ff
cresc.
f non ligato
ff
78
p
cresc.
p
cresc.
p
cresc.
p
cresc.

82
ri - tar - dan - do
cresc.
a tempo.
a tempo
90
cresc.
99
cresc.
107
espressivo
cresc.
rf
113

118
cresc.
cresc.
cresc.
cresc.
f
f
f
f
123
p non ligato
p non ligato
p dolce
p
128
più cresc.
più cresc.
più cresc.
più cresc.
dim.
dim.
dim.
dim.
teneramente
p
p
teneramente
pp
pp
pp
pp
133
cresc.
cresc.
cresc.
cresc.
f
f
f
f
137
sf
sf
sf
sf
sf
sf
sf
sf

141
145
151
157
161
cresc.
più f
morendo
sempre pp
pp
cresc.

Allegro ma non tanto.
11
21
1.
2.
25
29
39

48
cresc.
58
67
dim.
pp
76
86

96
cresc.
f
p
1.
2.
pp
101
semp.
pp
cresc.
110
Fine.
p
f
cresc.
120
p dol.
130
p

140
pp
sempre stacc.
pp
pp
sempre stacc.
150
sempre stacc.
cresc.
p
cresc.
cresc.
dol.
p
sempre stacc.
cresc.
p
159
sempre stacc.
sempre stacc.
sempre stacc.
169
poco cresc.
sempre stacc.
p
poco cresc.
p
poco cresc.
p
semp. stacc.
poco cresc.
p
semp. stacc.
179

189
cresc.
p
sempre stacc.
cresc.
sempre stacc.
198
f
p
208
L'istesso tempo.
221
p dol.
poco
a
230
dim.
più p
pp
D.C. al Fine.

Heiliger Dankgesang eines Genesenen an die Gottheit, in der lydischen Tonart.
(Canzona di ringraziamento offerta alla divinità da un guarito, in modo lidico.)

NB. Die deutschen Ueberschriften sind von Beethovens Hand, die italienischen von fremder Hand im Originalmanuscript geschrieben.

50
tr
pp
cresc.
55
rf
p
61
cresc.
66
p cantabile espressivo
74
cresc.

Molto adagio.
80
p
più p
pp
88
cresc.
p
96
cresc.
f
104
112
Andante.
ten.
f

118
ten.
cresc.
123
ten.
128
cresc.
135
pp
139
rf
pizz.

144
6
pp
arco
147
cresc.
rf
151
p
tr
158
163
più p

Molto adagio.
168
Mit innigster Empfindung.
(Con intimissimo sentimento.)
Mit innigster Empfindung.
(Con intimissimo sentimento.)
Mit innigster Empfindung
(Con intimissimo sentimento)
Mit innigster Empfindung.
(Con intimissimo sentimento.)
174
cresc.
179
dim.
p più p
pp
cresc.
185
cresc.
190
dim.

196
p
più p
pp
cresc.
rf
204
più p
pp
p
Alla Marcia, assai vivace.
f
sf
dol.
cresc.
6
11

16
21
attacca subito
cresc.
25
Più allegro.
ritard.
in tempo
espress.
32
immer geschwinder
accelerando
pp accelerando
cresc.
dim.
ritard.
Presto.
40
Poco adagio.
smorzando
attacca

Allegro appassionato.
espressivo
cresc.
rinf.
10
20
30
40

49
58
69
79
90
tr
p
cresc.
f
ff
sf
sempre ff
dim.
più p
pp
espressivo

100
cresc.
110
cresc.
120
130
dim.
più p
139
cresc.

148
157
dim.
più p
pp
166
espress.
cresc.
176
p espress.
186
arco
pizz.

196
205
215
226
236
cresc.
sempre ff
dim.
tr
f
sf
p
pp
ff

247
pp
sempre pp
sempre pp
sempre pp
pp
sempre pp
pp
259
pp
sempre pp
sempre pp
sempre pp
sempre pp
cresc.
poco
a
poco
pizz.
270
immer geschwinder.
accelerando
arco
Presto.
280
289
p

298
309
pp
321
pizz.
arco
cresc.
poco
a
poco
331
più cresc.
stacc.
dim.
341
p
più p
pp
tr
f
fp
dol.

353
non ligato
non ligato
363
pp
pp
pp
pp
373
cresc.
poco a poco
col punto d'arco
più cresc.
383
f
dim.
p
più p
393
pp
cresc.
tr
f
p
ff

To Johann Wolfmeier

String Quartet No. 16
in F Major, Op. 135
(1826)

33
cresc.
p
39
f
sf
44
pp
51
57

67
75
cresc.
f
p
82
poco ri - tar - dan - do
pizz.
arco
piu.
89
a tempo
sempre p
94

99
cresc.
sf
104
cresc.
arco
pizz.
110
120
127

133
cresc.
p
sfp
138
sf
f
143
pp
149
pp
155
f

161
169
175
180
188
cresc.
al f
sf
pizz.
arco

Vivace.
p
pp
dim.
cresc.
f
pp
12
23
35
46

57
1.
2.
dim.
p sempre
più p
pp
f
67
fp
78
cresc.
89
p
102
dim.

113
pp
cresc.
123
fp
f
sempre p
134
cresc.
ff
144
sf
154

164
174
dim.
p
sempre
più p
184
pp
ppp
193
meno p
205
pp

217
dim.
p
pp
cresc.
cresc.
229
f
dim.
pp
240
251
cresc.
dim.
262
p sempre
più p
pp
f
1.
2.
dim.
p
più p
pp

Lento assai, cantante e tranquillo.
p cresc.
solto voce
cresc.
dim.
rfz
Più lento.
pp
Tempo I.
10
19
26
33

40
ten.
ten.
semplice
45
cresc.
poco
a
poco
50
p
cresc.
rfz
dim.
pp
ritardando
DER SCHWER GEFASSTE ENTSCHLUSS.
Grave.
Muss es sein?
Allegro.
Es muss sein!
Es muss sein!
Grave ma non troppo tratto.
p
cresc.
f

Adagio.
Allegro.
dim.
p cresc.
pp
cresc.

61
cresc.
p
72
f
più f
ff
sf
1.
80
2.
86
sempre
92
sempre p
104
pp

116
cresc.
p
128
pp
139
tr
150
dim.
ritar
dando
in tempo
p cresc.
161
Grave ma non troppo tratto.
ff
sf
f

167
dim.
p
cresc.
f
poco rit.
Allegro.
174
p dolce
sf
185
sempre f
197
sempre p
208
cresc.

220
cresc.
232
cresc.
più f
1.
Si repete la seconda parte al suo piacere.
2.
243
Poco adagio.
Tempo I.
pizz.
255
arco
266
sempre pp

To Archduke Rudolph

Grosse Fuge

in B-flat Major, Op. 133

(1826)

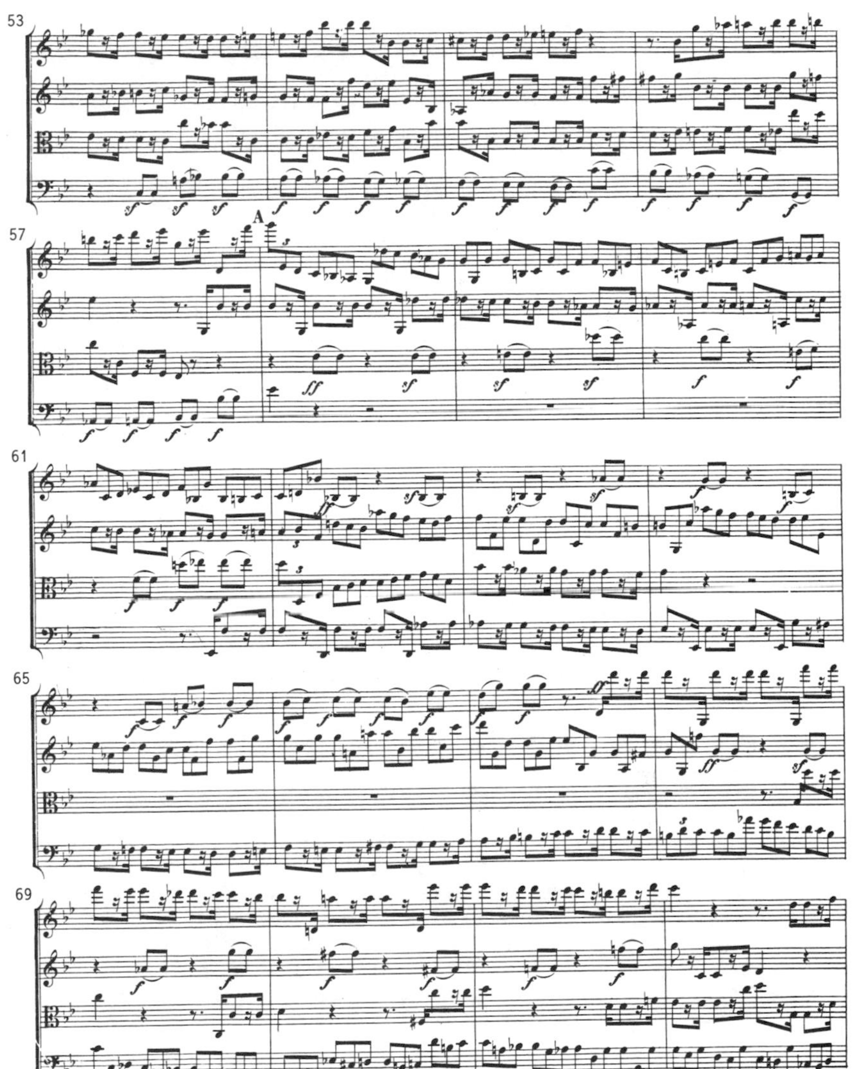
53
A
57
61
65
69

73
77
B
81
85
89

93
97
101
105
109
C
f
sf
ff

113
117
121
125
129

133
137
D
141
145
ben marcato
149

153
157
ben tenuto
Meno mosso e moderato.
sf
pp
ben tenuto
161
166
sempre pp
171

176
pp
pp
182
sempre pp
sempre pp
188
194
200

205
E
sempre pp
sempre pp
sempre pp
sempre pp
211
217
cresc.
cresc.
cresc.
cresc.
f
f
f
f
223
dim.
più dim.
dim.
più dim.
dim.
più dim.
dim.
più dim.
228
p
più
p
pp
p
più
p
pp
p
più
p
pp
p
più
p
pp

233
Allegro molto e con brio.
tr
ff
fp
p
241
249
258
267
F
cresc.
sf

276
ben marcato
285
ben marcato
293
ben marcato
302
ben marcato
311

320
G
328
336
345
353
H

360
367
374
381
389

396
tr
I
404
414
ff
p
423
432
sf

441
449
459
468
477
K

485
493
Meno mosso e moderato.
499
505
511
poco a poco sempre più allegro ed accelerando il tempo
dim.
poco a poco sempre più allegro ed accelerando il tenpo

523
più p
pp
533
Allegro molto e con brio.
fp
541
549
558
L
cresc.

567
dim.
cresc.
576
dim.
585
sempre pp
594
pizz.
603
cresc.
M
arco

611
sempre pp
sempre pp
sempre pp
sempre pp
624
cresc.
cresc.
cresc.
cresc.
f
f
f
f
633
p cresc.
p cresc.
p cresc.
p cresc.
641
f
dim.
cresc.
649
dim.
p
più p
pp

657
Allegro.
ff
Meno mosso e moderato.
pp
Allegro molto e con brio.
ff
sf
668
f
673
tr
683
dim.
p
più p
pp
dim
695
N
tr

END OF EDITION